MEGA MINIBEASTS

picthall and gunzi

an imprint of Award Publications Limited

BE A SUPER SPOTTER

Study these pictures and look out for them as you read this book. Can you answer the super spotter questions?

Whose eyes are these?

Who's enjoying their lunch?

Whose disguise is this?

Whose legs are these?

ISBN 978-1-909763-56-2

First published 2021

Written by: Nina Filipek and Sophie Giles

Images: Shutterstock.com (Ian Grainger, nednapa, anek.soowannaphoom, Dr Morley Read, Eugene Kalenkovich, Dobermaraner, Henrik Larsson, StudioSmart, Lenka_X, Tomatito, Maryna Pleshkun, Nneirda, Tomatito, Belikova Oksana, Lisa-S, John Griffiths, Sebastian Janicki, Elliotte Rusty Harold, Andrea Mangoni, Siriporn Schwendener, Ethan Daniels, cbpix, by pap, Boriboon Chutikaseam, Halyna Parinova, Belle Ciezak, Vyaseleva Elena, Martin Pelanek, Ezume Images, Cattlaya Art, DihooTro, Oh suti, Paul Reeves Photography, Dave Hansche, lomiso, Adisorn Maksunthorn, Zmrzlinar, Graham R Prentice, Kirsanov Valeriy Vladimirovich, Pan Xunbin, hagit berkovich, photolinc, Eric Isselee, jps, Henrik Larsson, Istomina Olena, Bonnie Taylor Barry, Sarah2, alslutsky, Cristina Romero Palma, Paul Looyen, r.classen, IrinaK, MongPro, arka38, Karel Gallas, Kletr, Butterfly Hunter, irin-k, asawinimages, anat chant, skydie, Protasov AN, Africa Studio, alslutsky, Aleksandar Dickov, ppl, Matee Nuserm, Irina Kozorog, Gaijineyeview, 24Novembers, frank60, nicemyphoto, Elizaveta ckaia)

21-968 1

Printed in China

CONTENTS

MEGA MINIBEASTS

Insects, worms, snails and spiders are all types of minibeast. There are more minibeasts living on Earth than any other group of animals. Among the strongest is the rhinoceros beetle, a type of stag beetle. It can lift 850 times its own weight – that would be like a human adult lifting 10 elephants all at once!

What is an insect?

Insects have six legs, one or two pairs of wings, and a body that is made up of three sections: a head, a thorax and an abdomen. They also have feelers (or 'antennae'). Examples of insects include ants, beetles, bees and wasps.

Wasp

Feeler (antenna)

Thorax

Wing

Leg

Abdomen

Wing case

How does it use its horn?

Hard body on the outside – called an exoskeleton

Mega old

Some minibeasts, such as this eight-legged harvestman, have been around for hundreds of millions of years – since before the dinosaurs!

Horn used for digging and to fight other males over food

Earthworm

Other types of minibeast

Spiders, centipedes, millipedes, slugs, snails and worms are all examples of minibeasts that are not insects. They have different body types and features to insects. For example, spiders have eight legs rather than six like insects do, and worms have no legs at all.

Head

Feeler (antenna)

Clever minibeasts

Minibeasts can communicate with one another, and often work together to survive. Bees do a 'waggle dance' to tell other bees where they have found pollen. Some ants are able to form living bridges to cross small streams or gaps.

Rhinoceros beetle

Leg

These ants are working together to bridge a gap

MINIBEAST HOMES

Bee nest

Some minibeasts are so tiny that many of them can live under a single petal. Others build homes where thousands can live together. A bee colony can be home to over 60,000 bees, and a termite mound may have millions of termites living inside!

Busy beehive

The bee nest on the right hangs from a tree. It is made up of hexagonal cells, which form storage boxes for eggs, larvae, pollen and nectar. Worker bees make the cells out of wax.

Worker bees bring pollen and nectar to the nest

Wasps chew up wood fibres to build large, papery nests like this

Wasp nest

Instead of building a home, these tiny red spider mites live on a flower

Anthill

Anthills are mounds of earth that are created when ants dig out their underground nests. Each anthill is part of a colony, similar to a village. They are joined to other anthills by underground tunnels.

Hexagonal (six-sided) cells make up the honeycomb

Termite mounds

Termites build massive mounds using soil, saliva and their own droppings! Inside, there are many tunnels and chimneys to allow air to flow though. The king and queen termites live deep underground, below the mound, where it is safest.

What are the cells in a bee nest used for?

SWIMMERS AND SKATERS

Some minibeasts, such as tadpoles, water snails, water boatmen and great diving beetles, live in streams and ponds. Their bodies are specially shaped to suit living in water. They swim to the surface to take in air, which they trap under their wings to use while swimming underwater.

Great diving beetle

Wing case

Water boatman

This minibeast gets its name from its long back legs that look like a boat's oars. It uses them to swim through the water.

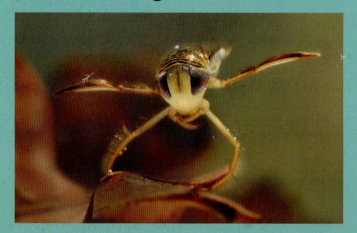

Can you point to?

a back leg   an eye   mouth

How does this beetle breathe underwater?

Compared to land beetles, diving beetles have flatter bodies, which help them to swim better

Antenna

Pond skaters detect their prey through vibrations on the water's surface

Eye

Shorter front legs for grasping prey

Strong back legs for swimming

Pond skater

Pond skaters seem to walk on water due to the water-repellent hairs on their feet. They use their middle legs to move themselves across the surface of the water.

In a spin

Whirligig beetles spin on the water's surface as they search for food. They have two pairs of eyes: one underneath for looking underwater, and one on top to watch the surface.

Upper eyes

LOTS OF LEGS

Some minibeasts have lots and lots of legs, but it is a myth that centipedes have 100 legs and millipedes have 1,000. On average, centipedes have 70 legs. Millipedes have many more than that. The giant African millipede has between 300 and 400 legs and can grow up to 40 centimetres long!

Can you point to?

 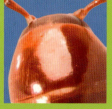 

legs   a head   segments

Body parts

Centipedes and millipedes have bodies that are divided into parts (called 'segments'). Centipedes have one pair of legs per segment and millipedes have two.

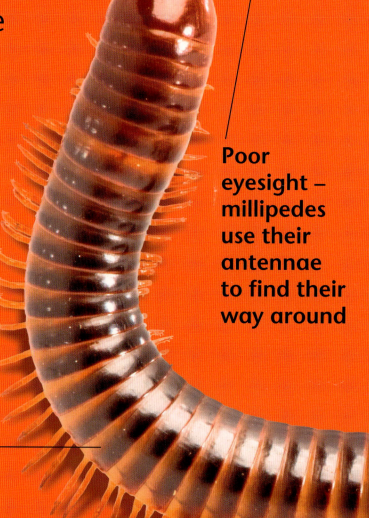

Millipede

Poor eyesight – millipedes use their antennae to find their way around

Each segment has four legs, two on each side

Millipedes are burrowers

A millipede's legs are good for burrowing in the soil, where it feeds mainly on dead leaves. When threatened, a millipede will curl up and release a horrible-smelling liquid.

What's the difference?	Centipedes	Millipedes
	Eat meat	Eat plants
	Run fast	Move slowly
	Bite	Do not bite

Speedy centipedes

Millipedes are slow-moving but centipedes are fast. Most centipedes are venomous and are fierce hunters of other minibeasts, such as spiders, worms and cockroaches. Being quick helps them catch their prey.

Centipede

What is prey?

Animals that are eaten by other animals are called 'prey'.

Legs for burrowing

What do millipedes eat?

SLITHERING AND SLIDING

Some minibeasts have wings to fly or legs to run. Earthworms, slugs and snails don't have wings or legs. Instead, they have developed different ways of moving. They wriggle, slither and slide. Earthworms eat their way through the soil. Slugs and snails move on their own slime!

Slimy slugs and sliding snails

Slugs and snails are creatures we call 'gastropods'. A snail has a shell and a slug does not, but they move in the same way. Underneath the body is a 'foot' that releases slime. Slugs and snails slide along the ground on this bed of slime. They can also climb by using their foot like a sucker!

Sea slugs

Sea slugs are found in the ocean in all colours, shapes and sizes. Their colours help to stop predators from eating them. The fronds on their backs are gills for breathing.

Garden slug

Hard shell

Eyespots at the tips of the tentacles sense light

Short tentacles smell food

Garden snail

Tough tongue
Slugs and snails don't have teeth like ours. Instead, they have a 'radula'. It is a bit like a cheese grater and rips and shreds food.

Earthworms
An earthworm's body it made up of many segments. It moves by using its muscles to shorten and lengthen its body. Tiny bristles along its body stop it from sliding backwards as it moves through the soil.

Mouth

Segment

Foot oozes slime and moves the snail along

Tail end

SUPER SENSES

We have two eyes, each with one lens. Some insects have many eyes. Others have only two eyes, but many lenses in each one. Dragonflies have the biggest eyes of all minibeasts, with 30,000 lenses. Their huge eyes almost cover the whole of their head. This allows them to see in all directions at once (except directly behind), but not in great detail.

Can you point to?

legs   head   eye pattern

Zoom in

This jumping spider has four green eyes. The two eyes on the outside are used to sense movement. The middle eyes work like binoculars to magnify what the spider can see.

What makes a dragonfly's eyes different to ours?

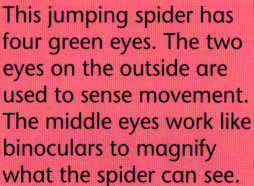

The dragonfly can spot movement much quicker than we can

Antenna

Feeling smells

Using their antennae, minibeasts can smell food and other creatures, which helps them find a mate, or avoiding being eaten. A male moth can smell a female 6 kilometres away!

The male moth has feathered antennae

Eye with 30,000 lenses

Tasting with their feet

Some insects, such as butterflies and flies, can taste with their feet! Tiny hair-like sensors underneath their feet 'taste' what the minibeast is walking on.

A fly tasting an orange

Mouth

Hearing with their knees

Some minibeasts have ears in unusual places. Crickets have 'ears' just below their knees. They are tiny holes that are smaller than the point of a pin!

FIERCE FEEDERS

Praying mantises catch other minibeasts with their long front legs, then eat them alive! Larger mantises can even catch frogs and birds. These predators sit and wait with their front legs held high until a victim comes within reach, and then they grab it with lightning speed!

Eyes that see like binoculars

Jaws

Praying mantis

Long front legs lined with sharp spikes

What is a predator?

Animals that hunt and eat other animals are called 'predators'.

Giant redheaded centipede

The giant redheaded centipede can grow to up to 20 centimetres long. It uses its long feelers to find food (usually insects and spiders) but it can also catch larger prey, such as mice, frogs and even small snakes! It grabs its prey using its back legs then injects it with venom from the pincer-like legs just behind the head, called 'forcipules'.

Centipedes are the only insects that have forcipules

Forcipules

Meeting a sticky end

This spider is waiting in the centre of its web for a flying insect to get stuck on the sticky threads. The spider will then wrap its prey in the same silk it makes to build its web before eating it!

Can you point to?

an eye   a feeler   a wing case

What do mantises eat?

Strong back legs for walking

Fire ants

These ants only sting only to defend their territory. Their sting feels like a burn you would get from a flame. Stings from fire ants can kill small animals, and cause pain and swelling in humans.

Stag beetle

The 'antlers' on male stag beetles make them look incredibly fierce. They are used to attract a mate and to wrestle other male stag beetles. The beetle can pinch with them but they are quite weak and are harmless to humans.

BIG APPETITES

What a minibeast eats depends on the type of mouth it has. Beetles and ants have strong jaws for biting leaves and catching prey. Some minibeasts suck up their food. Butterflies drink flower nectar through a long spiral tube called a 'proboscis'.

Antennae

Sephisa princeps butterfly

Proboscis, for drinking nectar

Caterpillars

Caterpillars are the larvae of butterflies and moths and have huge appetites. They mainly eat leaves and can cause a lot of damage to plants.

Locust

Locusts will sometimes breed and swarm in massive numbers, especially when there has been wet weather followed by a drought. In just a few hours, a swarm of hungry locusts can strip a field bare of all plants.

Locusts' powerful jaws easily cut through grass, leaves and other vegetation

What does a butterfly feed on?

Dung beetle

Every day, this beetle eats its own weight in dung (or poo)! It collects its own dung and that of other minibeasts and rolls it into a ball. It can push a ball of dung that is over 1,100 times its weight – which is like a 10-year-old child pushing more than 30 polar bears!

Stay away!

Some minibeasts are brightly coloured. This can be to attract a mate, or for camouflage, but often the colours are a warning to predators that the creature tastes bad or is poisonous if eaten!

This saddleback caterpillar has spines that can release venom!

Wings

Leg

MOST DANGEROUS

A few minibeasts are dangerous not just to other minibeasts and animals but to humans, too. Most are venomous spiders or scorpions. The North American black widow spins a web to catch its prey, and then injects it with venom. Only the females have mouth parts long enough to bite a human.

How many legs does a spider have?

Red marking

Black body

Black widow spider

Sydney funnel-web spider

This spider lives in Australia and is the most dangerous in the world. A bite from a male funnel-web spider could kill a human if they aren't given antivenom. Antivenom is a medicine to treat venomous bites and stings. Different types of antivenom are used for bites from different creatures.

Can you point to?

red marking

jaws

legs

Deathstalker scorpion

This scorpion is one of the most deadly minibeasts. It grabs its prey and crushes it, before stinging it with paralysing venom from its tail. The deathstalker attacks incredibly quickly, flicking its tail at 1.3 metres per second!

Jointed leg

Jaws

Mosquito

Proboscis

To deter insects from biting, we can use insect repellents on our skin and clothing

Mosquito

Only female mosquitoes bite. They use their proboscis (a tube-like mouthpiece) to pierce the skin and suck blood from the animals they land on. This 'bite' can be painful and often makes the skin around it red and itchy. Mosquito bites can be dangerous to humans, as they can spread diseases such as malaria.

GROWING AND CHANGING

Many minibeasts hatch from eggs and look just like their parents, only smaller. Because they have a hard outer skeleton, as they grow, they moult (shed their hard casing) and grow a new, bigger one. But some young minibeasts change so much that they look totally different by the time they are adults, such as when a caterpillar turns into a butterfly. This change is called 'metamorphosis'.

What do caterpillars eat?

From egg to butterfly

1. Egg (4–10 days)
The swallowtail butterfly lays her eggs on a leaf

2. Larval stage (3–4 weeks)
The caterpillar hatches from the egg and begins to eat the leaves.

3. Pupal stage (10–20 days)
The caterpillar changes into a pupa, also known as a 'chrysalis', before breaking out as a butterfly.

4. Adult (6–14 days)
It flies away to find a mate and lay its own eggs, and the lifecyle begins again!

1
2
3
4

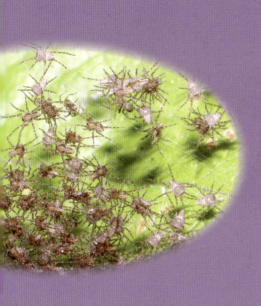

Spiderlings
When baby spiders (called 'spiderlings') hatch from their eggs, they look like tiny copies of their parents.

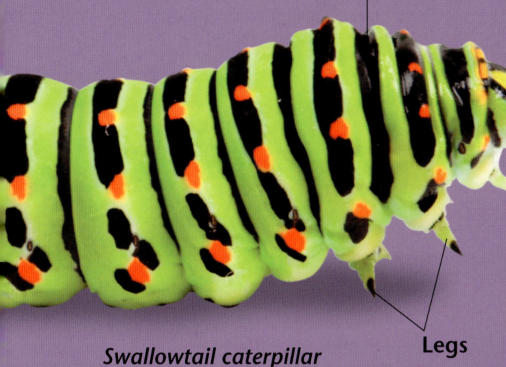

Soft body

Swallowtail caterpillar

Legs

Damsel nymphs
The damselfly lays her eggs on water plants. The nymphs that hatch from the eggs eat water fleas. As they grow, they shed their skin up to 15 times. When fully grown, they climb out of the water and fly away.

Strong jaws

An ant's life
Like a butterfly, an ant starts life as an egg and hatches as a white grub. It is fed by worker ants until it spins a cocoon around itself, becoming a pupa. Inside the cocoon, the ant changes into its adult form and emerges fully grown.

An ant and her eggs

A worker ant protects the pupae

SUPER-SIZED

The Atlas moth is the biggest moth in the world. From wing tip to wing tip it can measure up to 30 centimetres. That's as long as a school ruler! It can only survive for a couple of weeks before it dies because it doesn't eat after it emerges from its cocoon.

Atlas moth

Antenna

Body

Mega stick insect

In 2014 a scientist searching in the south of China found the longest stick insect in the world. It measured 62.4 centimetres! Despite its size, it can still hide easily from its enemies as it looks so much like a stick!

Largest beetle

The Titan beetle is the largest beetle in the world. Titan beetles live in tropical rainforests in South America. Unfortunately, as their rainforest homes are destroyed for timber, they are becoming endangered.

Atlas moth caterpillars grow to 12 centimetres long! Its name in Cantonese means 'snake's head'.

Can you point to?

antennae markings body

Can you see the snake's head pattern on its wing tips?

Wing

Teeny tiny

Some minibeasts are so small that they can't easily be seen. Fleas are only 1–3 millimetres long. Using a magnifying glass or microscope can help you to see them clearly.

Heaviest insect

The giant weta from New Zealand is the heaviest insect on Earth. It weighs more than a mouse, and has to run like one, too, as it is too heavy to fly or jump. Wetas that are kept in zoos like to eat carrots!

MASTERS OF DISGUISE

Some minibeasts use camouflage to avoid being seen or eaten. They have colours and patterns on their bodies or wings to match their natural habitat. This can help them to hide from predators. Other minibeasts use disguise to catch their prey!

Blue morpho

The blue morpho butterfly is a beautiful blue on one side of its wings, but on the other side it has dark spots that look like eyes. The spots trick its predators into thinking it is something big and scary!

Antennae

Blue morpho butterfly

Body

Blue morpho butterfly

The blue morpho's closed wings look like 'eyes'

Why do creatures use disguise?

Leg

Bright blue
open wings

Flower mantis

This mantis is trying to look like a
flower. It sits very still and waits
silently for an insect to walk by and
then pounces on it with open jaws!

**The mantis's
head,
body and
legs look
like flower
petals**

Stick around

With its colouring, thin body and
long legs, a stick insect looks just
like a stick! This camouflage makes
it hard for predators to see it.

Leafwing butterfly

The leafwing butterfly pretends to be a leaf!
Its colour and markings make it look just
like the plant that it lives on, so other
creatures don't easily notice it.

**The leafwing butterfly's
closed wings look like
a dry leaf**

27

RECORD BREAKERS

The globe skimmer dragonfly holds the record for the longest insect flight. Millions of dragonflies migrate thousands of kilometres from southern India to Africa each year. Their journey is over 7,000 kilometres long and takes them four to five months! They glide on the wind, feeding on smaller insects on the way.

Two pairs of wings

Long body

Can you point to?

body

legs

a wing

Noisy neighbours

There are over 3,000 known species of cicada. They are the loudest insects in the world. At around 100 decibels, the mating calls these insects make is louder than a motorbike!

Cicadas make their sound by flexing muscles to repeatedly buckle their ribs – like how you can bend a ruler to make a sound

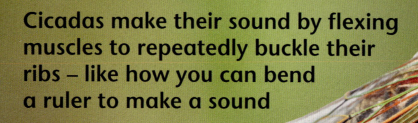

Midges, such as this sand fly, have the fastest wingbeat speed of any insect – an incredible 1,946 beats per second!

How long is a globe skimmer dragonfly's migration?

Globe skimmer dragonfly

Legs tucked up during flight

Monarch butterfly

From as far north as Canada, monarch butterflies migrate south to the warmer weather of Mexico each year, covering around 4,000 kilometres. They have the longest migration of any butterfly species. Loss of food sources and habitat is a great threat to these fragile creatures.

How do these butterflies know the way?

They use the position of the sun to know which direction to fly. However, researchers believe that their antennae contain a compass and biological clock, which also helps to guide them.

NATURE'S HELPERS

When a bee visits a flower, pollen sticks to its body and rubs off onto other flowers that the bee visits. This is called 'pollination' and helps the flowers to form fruit or seeds. Without bees and other pollinating insects, such as wasps, hoverflies, beetles and butterflies, we would not have so many kinds of fruit and vegetables!

Wonderful worms

When earthworms burrow through the soil they make holes that fill with water and air. Plants use this water and air to help them grow. Earthworms eat dead plants, and their poo makes the soil better for new plants to grow!

How do bees help us?

Feeds on nectar and pollen

Brilliant beetles

Some beetles can be useful because they eat other insects that are harmful to the vegetables we grow for food. Ladybirds are also helpful because they feed on mites and other bugs that eat our flowers! If they didn't do this, we would have fewer flowers.

Bumblebee

Pollen sticks to its body and legs

Ant-astic!

An ant can carry up to 50 times its own weight. That's like you carrying a car in your teeth! Scientists are studying ants to find out what it is that makes them so strong, so that we can make robots that are as strong as ants.

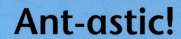

Ants are highly organised and work together in colonies

Master recyclers

Flies are nature's cleaners! They eat up food waste and animal poo. Without them, our world would be a much dirtier place!

GLOSSARY

Antennae – a pair of sensory 'feelers' on the head of an insect or minibeast.

Camouflage – patterns or markings on an animal's body that help it to blend in with its surroundings.

Cocoon – a silky case made by the larvae of some insects as they enter the pupa stage of their metamorphosis.

Colony – a group of animals of the same type living closely together.

Endangered – when an animal or plant is at risk of becoming extinct (dying out).

Larva – the young of a creature that transforms when it becomes an adult. Tadpoles are the larvae of frogs.

Lens – part of the inside of an eye that focuses light and helps an animal to see.

Migration – when an animal travels a long distance to a habitat with a better climate for finding food or breeding.

Metamorphosis – when an animal changes completely as it becomes an adult, for example when a caterpillar turns into a butterfly.

Nectar – a sweet liquid made by plants. Bees use nectar to make honey.

Nymph – a young form of an insect that does not change as it matures to adulthood (unlike larvae).

Pollen – a fine powder (usually yellow) on the male parts of plants.

Predator – an animal that hunts and eats other animals.

Prey – an animal that is caught or hunted and eaten by another animal.

Proboscis – a long, flexible tube for sucking up food.

Pupa – the stage between the larva and adult form of an insect, such as a cocoon or chrysalis.

Venomous – being able to inject a substance (venom) by a bite or sting, for protection or to kill prey.

INDEX